Living Ones Originality

ANITA KONGARI

First Published in January 2022

ISBN: 978-93-5472-449-7

BLUEROSE PUBLISHERS

www.bluerosepublishers.com

info@bluerosepublishers.com

+91 8882 898 898

Cover Design:

Vanshika Baranwal

Typographic Design:

Ilma Mirza

Distributed by: BlueRose, Amazon, Flipkart

Dedication

I dedicate this book to my late parents. My mother who has taught me to be kind and father to serve selflessly with the God given talents.

Preface

I am sitting at the stream surrounded by beautiful nature. I awe much to this stream because it has soothed my painful heart especially after my father's death in 2020. I listen to the lovely chirping of the birds and the gentle flow of the stream. I recall the time when I started writing poems. It is just few years back that I have started. The first poem that I wrote was a Hero within. After writing this poem I became aware of the hero within me in the form of a unique poet. I read this poem again and again and I felt good and inspired. Eventually I began writing poems on different themes.

A word of appreciation works miracle. Whenever somebody appreciated me I felt happy and grew as a better person. As a teacher I realize more and more the need to appreciate and encourage the students because it transforms them into better persons. So keeping this in mind I wrote appreciative poems which I gave them on their birthdays. They were very happy.

To respect others I have learnt from my mother in my early childhood. She treated everyone with respect. I suppose that's the reason she was respected too. I remember one incident. In the village we have black smith living. One day an elderly man came to our house for some work. My mother gave him a chair to sit but he refused to sit thinking of himself as a low caste. My mother requested him to sit. I could see on his face the reflection of being accepted as he was. What a joy!

As a teenager I was appreciated for my good personality by my family and others as well. I felt happy and special but still I suffered from low self esteem to some extent. I think because I was compared with my elder sister who was better than me in studies. My father may not have done intentionally but I was wounded. Now that I am grown up as an adult woman I appreciate and encourage little Anita within me when she does things well. She feels a sense of confidence.

I am a nature lover. I enjoy time of solitude. When I am stressed out I go for a walk in the wood and listen to the beautiful singing of the birds. I walk on the soft green grass and feel it's coolness. I look up the lovely blue sky and observe the birds flying.Gradually it soothes my heart and I feel at ease. In the night before going to bed I recall the blessings of the day and write down at least five of them. I feel blessed, happy and look forward to live for another day. This attitude of daily gratitude enables me to live my life happily in the midst of high tide and low tide of daily life.

Each passing day is a reminder for me about the shortness of life. The more I become aware of this reality I try to live my life meaningfully. I reflect on my originality and the purpose of my life. I have seen many deaths in my family. My beloved mother passed away in 2014. I was in Mumbai. My father gave me the news of her death. My heart was broken. I started my journey the same morning but could not be there for the funeral because the train was late. I rang them up and told them to go ahead with the funeral service because they had been waiting for me. In the train I cried and cried. However I made myself very brave to accept her home going. As a result I was a strong support to my emotional father who was very close to her. After a day or two many people met me. Whoever met me spoke of her goodness especially about her loving kindness.In 2020 my dear father expired. It was very painful but I was fortunate to be there beside him till his last breath. What consoles me is his peaceful going after one and a half day of painful suffering. As he was nearing his last breath he kissed the cross of his rosary and closed his eyes for eternity leaving behind his legacy of tender love and selfless service to the country as C.R.P.F and as a member of the village Panchayat samiti. On the day of his funeral there were many people from my village as well as from the neighbouring villages. He was social and a wisdom figure for the younger generation in the

Panchayat samiti. On his funeral day the atmosphere was very sad for us and for the entire village because he was a significant person in the village and an active member in the church unit. As we were returning from the funeral I thought of my own funeral and a question came to my mind. That was, what will people remember me for when I die? All the other things can pass away but not death. Death is certain for all of us. This reality is fearful but at the same time enables me to live my originality fully as a teacher and a writer. Though I am an ordinary teacher I try to live this profession as fully as I can by encouraging and appreciating the students along with imparting value based academic knowledge. Ever since I have become aware of the poet within me I desire to touch, inspire and enrich the readers through my simple poetry. Let me be a little drop of change in the world through the God given gifts to me. May I leave behind a legacy of selfless service through the service of education and through the passion of writing poetry. Dear readers as you read may you become aware of your originality. I respect your uniqueness. There is no other you in the world and no one can play your role except you. Keeping this in mind I encourage you to contribute to the world through your unique God given talents and leave behind your legacy. Remember you are special.

Acknowledgements

I render my deep gratitude to God for giving me the gift of writing. I thank my family, near and dear ones for their love, care and support. I also thank my close friend across the sea for his constant support and encouragement to reach to the stage of publication.Finally I express my heartfelt gratitude to my publishers at Blue Rose for their guidance, trust and hard work to bring this book to the stage of completion. I have experienced them as dedicated team who are approachable. And to you my dear readers I thank you in anticipation for choosing and taking time to read this book. I hope you will receive something from it.

With gratitude & care,

Anita K.

Table of Content

Two in one

I was born to my hopeful parents after some years of their wedding.

Different was I as years later narrated by my emotional mother who knew not how to fight with the traditional society.

Both my parents were unhappy and dissatisfied with my arrival.

They heard my cry which was thunder storming to their unfulfilled heart.

They were in battle with whether to accept me or not.

However mother's hearts are great as felt by many.

Closely held was I to her pumping heart.

She was lost and left alone in the struggle of big decision to accept me.

My father was standing apart from her thinking of the society where I would be different.

The sweat of stress fell from his forehead in anxiety.

My grandparents arrived to see me.

There I was lying rapped neatly with a bundle of white clothes

Overwhelmed were they with the tears of joy until they saw my body part that was different.

I was having the signs of both male and female two in one.

Seeing this my grandmother fainted so much so that she was rushed to the ICU.

On the other hand my grandpa was filled with anger with his raised brow.

Dad was standing silently trying to take control of the whole situation.

Though tiny unable to see clearly and speak I felt the negative atmosphere sweeping through all over my body.

How pained I felt as I lay in bed next to my fear filled mother whose touch was numbed and cold like ice cubes.

Wanted to cry loudly but I sobbed deeply taking control of the sensitive moments as a one day few minutes old baby.

That was like an earthquake to go through just out of my mother's secure womb.

I was brought home not with joy but uncertainty.

Before we stepped in our neighbours peeped me.

Their touch and look was not acceptable to my soft and sensitive skin.

As I was laid in bed we heard the shout of a group of people saying this baby belongs to us.

My mother was filled with the fear of separation.

I was closely held in my father's arm for the first and the last time.

I could hear his heart beat as I leaned against his chest.

That was the last day of my life with my family at the age of eight days old baby.

I was taken to the home of so called the third gender.

What a rejoicing over my arrival in their midst.

I felt loved, special and accepted as I am.

But something was still missing within me.

That was the tender love of my dear mother and father.

Eventually I grew up into an elegant person though I was of both the sexes.

I fell in love with a normal handsome young man in the train while begging for money.

But I could not express to him knowing of the reality of rejection.

Buried deep within this burning love for him I continue to live my life of a third gender.

No one knows what emotional pain I go through except one who created me.

I beg you to be respectful when I pass by on the road, train and in all the public places.

Emotionally I am just like you.

Different am I only in my physical appearance which is not my fault.

Wounded I feel when people laugh at me, at my looks and my life style.

Be respectful and kind to me this is what I request you nothing more nothing less.

When you do this you raise myself worth to live as a person of the third gender with dignity.

Originality

Peel the layers of skin and find your originality.

The originality of childhood like a free bird.

It soars and soars high above the blue sky.

There is no fear of falling down and the criticism of others.

You might have been told at different stages of your life as the one who knows nothing.

Do not fear.

That's not the reality and your originality.

The truth is you are capable of boundless things.

Remember the days of your childhood.

You loved swimming and won prizes.

Recall the moments where you won the trophy for preparing the girls to sing and dance to their hearts content.

It's your authentic self who has the capacity to prepare the girls to do their very best.

Relive the moments while teaching the girls in the class who naturally clapped their hands in appreciation for the best lesson you taught them.

It's your capability and your giftedness.

They are innocent and vulnerable people who tell the truth in simplicity.

So believe.

Cherish the time when you were whispered into your ears I love you, you are intelligent, special and loveable.

You were not lied.

You were genuinely appreciated by the person of authenticity.

Relish this moment and let this message sink deep into your soul and to your most inner being.

There is no falsehood in persons.

Each and every individual is blessed with the original self.

So I humbly ask you to look into yourself and introspect if there is any falsehood in your belief system of who you are.

I care for you thus I request you to peel layer by layer and find your true original self.

She is waiting to be discovered and to be of use.

May you be at peace with yourself and live happily making your originality in the service of human kind.

Self acceptance

When wounded in childhood accepting self is difficult in a growing age.

You were compared with others knowingly or unknowingly for not been able to study well and work well.

You felt sad and were broken.

You neglected yourself, your good qualities and your strengths.

Now that you are grown up you have the capacity to be a parent of that wounded child in you.

Listen to the cry of the inner child within you.

Give love, affirmation and appreciation to her.

Pat her gently on the shoulder when she does things well.

Encourage her and affirm her good qualities to do better in life.

Let her recall the moments when she was able to do things own her own.

Let her relive and cherish those moments of capabilities like being able to cook, sing, dance and teach etc.

Life alone will be her teacher as she grows and steps forward to the future.

When a child in you receives love, affirmation and encouragement she will be a new person.

The new world of possibilities will open for her.

She will never be afraid of anyone but find security within herself.

Gradually she will bloom and understand the brokenness of others and be a healing channel of growth to them.

Beautiful Me

I am as beautiful as a Princess.
My lovely eyes are as bright as a morning star.
My lips are as Pink as cherry blossom.
My hair is as lovely as flowers in the garden.
My cheeks are as beautiful as a tiny babe.
My nose is as sharp as a pencil.
Indeed I am beautiful!

My hands are as strong as an iron rod.
My palms are as delicate as a lamb.
My fingers are as creative as an artist.
My breasts are as rounded as an apple.
My stomach is as soft as wool.
My back is as awesome as the ocean.
My skin is as sensitive as the rising sun.
Indeed I am beautiful!

My legs are as long as a kangaroo.

My knees are as flexible as a bamboo stick.

My thighs are as pretty as a rose flower.

My toes are as wonderful as pearls.

My sole is as clean as a white cloth.

My buttocks are as attractive as a magnet.

My figure is as curvy as a beautiful woman.

Indeed I am beautiful.

Loving self

When I wake up in the morning I look at my face in the mirror.

I see brown patches on both the cheeks.

I feel upset and move away.

I stand again and see this time I look at it with a concern.

I touch my cheeks gently and lovingly.

I tell her how much I love her and want her to get well soon.

I apply some skin lightning cream.

I feel relaxed and hopeful that some day it will get healed.

I look at my beautiful brown eyes.

I thank God for blessing me with good eyesight.

Through which I can see myself, people and wonderful things in the universe.

I am able to read as many books I want to.

When I observe my eyebrows I see slight brown patches above it.

I go to the skin specialist who tells me the cause of it.

She gives me medicine to eat, apply and tells me to avoid the sun.

I come back home and start taking medicine and apply it with a childlike faith.

Months go by but no difference.

I feel sad and think of the past when I had a clean face.

I thank God for giving me clean cheeks and eyebrows for some years.

I try to accept my cheeks and eyebrow patches.

It is emotionally disturbing but I am learning to accept and befriend it.

When I wake up and look at in the mirror I say thank you God for creating all other parts of my body beautifully.

The attitude of gratitude for my other parts is enabling me to accept my entire self as I am.

I continue to treat it with my capacity and rest leave in the hands of God the healer who has healed the similar brown patch from my nose earlier.

I pray this too shall disappear one day and my cheeks and eyebrow be patches free.

What a miracle

I have a brain active and powerful than a computer.

I can think, feel and act.

I have two lovely eyes like that of a star.

I can see thousands of objects, people and animals and read books.

I have a life giving nose.

I can breathe in and breathe out with ease.

I have a cheerful mouth.

I can communicate, smile and eat delicious food.

I have a lovely set of teeth.

I can bite, smile and give joy to others.

I have a sensitive tongue.

I can taste and feed myself.

I have capable ears.

I can hear the sound of the people, wind, birds, animals, river, sea, music and my own heart beat.

I have a loving heart.

I can live and serve my family, friends and people at large.

I have machine like intestines.

I can digest food and be healthy.

I have healthy breasts.

I can feed, enable relationships and give life to new born babe.

I have two strong feet.

I can walk thousands of miles, work, play, run and dance.

I have delicate hands.

I can work, write, shake hands, wash, comb, sweep, cook, and do as many things I can.

My body parts are awesome.

It is a live laboratory which functions own it's own.

What a miracle!

God of artist

You are a wonderful artist.

When I look at a rising sun I get fascinated with the lovely rays around it.

It is simply spectacular.

In it I find your caring hand as I receive the warmth on my skin.

When I observe the setting sun I see the silver lining along with the colorful rays spreading far and wide.

I see the beauty of your creative hand.

Gradually it sets giving gentle warmth and soothing feeling to my heart.

When I am in the open air I see the birds flying high above.

I feel joy within me for giving them the energy and capability to fly wherever they wish to.

How beautifully you created them with different color, size and shapes.

I hear them singing melodiously bringing healing to my sad and lonely heart.

When I look up the sky I see thousands of twinkling stars arranged so beautifully in their permanent places.

It's heartwarming to see them in the dark night and in the moon light.

When I see the half moon I get curious by it's beautiful carved shape.

The full moon is incredible to see hanging up above the sky giving dim light to the earth which feels so romantic.

When I see the animals of different types I am inspired by their instinct to understand and care for each other when in need.

They are colorfully decorated.

Some looks as though they are being painted.

Their different shades are of fine color combination.

How thoughtfully and creatively you have made them.

When I look at myself and other humans I get awe struck with the unique creation of each person.

Woman in particular you concentrated on her figure and her beauty.

So elegantly you made her being curvy and in proper shape.

She is delicate and attractive in appearance.

Inwardly you made her strong to face hard situations.

When I look at a man I can only thank you for the pots of energy and strength with which you have blessed him.

He is the supporter of woman and the stronghold of the family in everyday life along with the woman.

You have made him handsome and intelligent with a warm heart.

God of artist your nature is to give freely always.

You have blessed each of us with the unique talents to be of service just like your created things which serve us in some way or the other.

Millions of gratitude I give to you the God of artist for creating everything creatively and elegantly.

Differently able student

We had a differently able student in our school.

Her name means 'work of art.'

She was unfortunately handicapped from birth.

Both her feet were weak so she moved around toddling.

She reached grade eight.

I was their class teacher.

I had a soft corner for her due to her disability.

She was calm and friendly by nature.

Her gasping ability was superb.

She taught to those who didn't understand the concept well.

Though she was lefty her handwriting was beautiful and eligible to read.

Her drawing described her painful life as she lost her mother at her young age.

She was in the age of physical changes.

She used to struggle but her companions were very helpful and sensitive specially her close friend.

She used to be fascinated to see cultural programe in the school.

I could see her desire to dance but could not.

However she enjoyed thoroughly to see other girls dancing happily.

There were many activities and competition conducted in the school.

She participated in handwriting, drawing and speech competition.

She won always.

One fine day we had a sport day in the school.

All the girls went happily on the playground.

She was sitting sadly under the tree.

I knew the reason of her sadness being seen in her eyes.

I taped on her shoulder and said to her.

Though you can't play you are good at many other things.

You have a good mind.

Your responses and answers in the class are unique and appealing.

You have a reflective heart.

The value that you share in the class at the end of the lesson is from the depth of your heart based on your daily experiences.

My dear you are unique and special.

Listening attentively to this her gloomy eyes beamed with joy and my heart was filled with joy too.

She started concentrating on the things that she was able to do.

She used to be either 1st or 2nd in the class.

She was an example to the other students of her class and the school.

Let your disability not become the stumbling block on your way of growth but be a ladder of success.

Elder sister

You were born to your simple and loving parents.

Mother taught you to have great faith in God.

Father to be courageous and soar to the heights in God given talents.

Active were you even though you grew up in the country away from all the educational sites.

You were multi-gifted at your tender age.

You helped mother in cooking and household chores with the at most care.

Delicious were your curry and vegetables which was eaten with delicacy.

Chapatti that you made was soft and tasty.

Clothes washed by you were clean as though they were just purchased from the shop.

You swept the house neat and clean.

Tidiness was your adorable friend.

You danced as flexible as lotus flower that sways with a gentle breeze.

Sang like a nightingale so much so that your voice was recorded and taken by a Belgian gentle man who loved it.

You knitted lovely sweaters and shawls for each family member with loving care.

Stitched handkerchief with gorgeous embroidery and sold to make pocket money as a collage going girl while your friends enjoyed a life of play.

You took tuition of math to unburden your parents for educational expenses.

Responsible were you as an elder sis of the family.

Your parents went through financial crises while you were in the collage.

You stood by them by taking more tuition of students who scored high marks in the exam.

How happy their parents were who gifted you with clothes and things at different occasions to show their gratitude for your hard work.

Desire you had to do B.ed but your parents were financially unstable at that time.

So you joined A.N.M which was your alternate choice and was affordable.

Your father had not enough money to pay fees so you took a break and went to Delhi to work as a maid for few months.

You worked there for six months in a wealthy family.

Out of love they called you Priti for they were happy with your neat work which you did responsibly.

You didn't disclose your true identity and education for a fear of being laughed at as a maid.

Son of their wanted to take an advantage of you thinking you were an ordinary, poor and uneducated girl.

I wonder how many uneducated and poor domestic workers are misused for whom I feel sorry.

But you were as cunning as a wolf who protected herself dignity with care.

Left their home after six months with enough money to pay fees and continued your training.

You are a good midwife nurse taking care of the pregnant women and helping them to deliver their babies.

It gives you joy to bring new life to the couples and to their families.

What a joy on your face when you hear the first cry of a baby.

Truly you are God's instrument who has successfully operated to bring forth life to many babies.

When they leave the hospital they show their gratitude to you by giving you sweets or some gifts.

Even outside the hospital you are greeted with affection and respect for your dedicated work as a midwife nurse.

Your name means ever blooming flower.

And you live up to your name my sis.

Sweet girl

The meaning of your name is sweet girl.

You are a sweet girl made in the image of your creator.

You are true to your name.

Indeed you have a charming personality.

Your smile is sweet like that of a small babe.

You spread joy through your smile.

You make the atmosphere lighter.

It is a beautiful quality.

Indeed your sweet smile is contagious.

You have a good voice.

Your voice is pleasant to hear.

Your expression while singing is beautiful.

Indeed your expression is natural.

You have the ability to dance.

You are flexible while dancing.

You capture the attention of the audience through your natural movement.

Indeed you dance to your heart's content.

You have the ability to pay attention in the class.

You try to revise the lesson daily.

Indeed you have the ability to pay attention.

You are able to play well.

It is good to see you playing in a team.

You try to build team spirit in the group.

Indeed you have the ability to work in a team.

As I wished her and handed over her this simple poem she felt very happy and surprised.

She sat quietly on her bench and read it smiling.

She thanked me for the gift of poem and more than that for the words of appreciation.

I was happy to add little joy to her day.

Turning point

There was a girl named which means cool.

She was friendly, loving and hyper just the opposite of her name.

She understood the lesson well but had a weakness of writing neatly.

Her handwriting was not readable easily even though she practiced daily.

Due to this she could get less mark compared to other students of her class.

One day while supervising the exam I commented saying your handwriting has improved a little.

Listening to this she felt very happy and thanked me.

From the next day onward she began writing little better and gradually her handwriting was eligible to read.

One word of appreciation was a miracle for her.

She was extraordinarily gifted with karate.

Her body was very flexible as well as strong.

She had a mountain of strength like that of a boy.

She was straight forward and did not fear to speak truth.

During the board exam she challenged naughty boys of her class.

They threatened her but she was not afraid of them because she knew karate well.

It was her weapon to safe guard herself from any danger.

She loved to take part in sports but had a fear of losing it.

One day during the running competition she was refusing to run.

She hid herself behind the girls.

I noticed her hiding so I went to her and asked her as to why she was hiding.

She said I am afraid to participate in the competition.

I said to her spontaneously to think positive and to run with all the strength that she has.

Time was set for the running competition.

They stood in their respective places.

Hearing get set go all of them ran speedily.

Cool ahead of all of them ran like a wind and stood first.

I was overjoyed to see her outbeating everyone.

At the end of the game she looked pleased.

She came and said to me teacher the positive thought works wonder.

Because of you I was able to come first.

From today I will never have fear in my mind to participate in the competition.

Honestly it was a turning point in her life from fear to bravery.

Intelligent and humble

Though poor you are gifted highly mother of the Vadas.

I admire your grasping ability of the content taught.

You are intelligent and humble.

Your sense of dressing is simple, neat and tidy always.

You are an example of being neat to the other students of the class.

In a spur of moment you learn things by heart.

Your retaining and memorizing capacity is admirable.

You have a natural leadership quality.

When the responsibility is given you never let anyone down.

In you I find trusted student no matter how hard the responsibility may be.

Your handwriting is neat and beautiful.

Books of yours are tended well.

It shows how much you love about learning and gaining knowledge.

Responses of yours are unique and well reflected.

Though young at age your vision of whom you want to be in future is clear.

You wish to be a skin specialist and to be a help to your finically unstable family is commendable.

Your body is slim and flexible.

While dancing your eyes and movements communicate it's meaning.

Every teacher looks for you for speech competition.

Modulation of your voice is good and clear.

Your gesture gives meaning of the speech that you present.

When I see you on the playground you are excited to play and win.

You play justly and when you win your eyes sparkle revealing your inner joy.

You encourage other players of your group to play well.

When they do well you pat them on their shoulder with joy which is contagious to the teachers around.

I pray that your wish be granted.

May you be of help to your family and to the world through your craft as a skin specialist in the future.

Daily gratitude

I wake up and thank God for giving me to see another day.

I wonder how my internal machines work on it's own as I respond to natures call before I begin a new day.

I feel fresh and light.

I wash and bathe with warm water.

My skin enjoys the clean warm water.

While bathing I praise thee for the gift of water and my body parts knitted so well.

After bath I do Surya Namaskar.

While doing it I breathe in and breathe out peace.

For few minutes I thank God for my body which is a gift to me.

I begin concentrating from head to toes.

I feel the wonder of being created as a unique person.

There is no other person in the world who resembles me and my talents.

After sometime I listen to the music or just listen to any sound that is around.

I hear the chirping of the birds who sit on the bamboo trees close to my house.

This lovely sound calms my mind and heart.

I then listen to my own breathing.

I become aware of the preciousness of my breath.

This gives me life and connects me with the life of God.

I can't see him but can feel him with the eyes of faith.

Once this breath stops I am dead.

So I consciously thank God for giving me a gift of life.

I then sit quietly for sometime thinking nothing.

During this moment I become aware of my existence and the role that I have to play in the world to be of service in some way.

I jot down one or two things in which I will serve others today through my profession.

For instance by giving a helping hand to an elderly person or appreciating someone.

I ask myself one question everyday.

How will I live my day today if it is a last day of my life?

This keeps me to be focused on the most important things.

I become more pleasant and kinder to others.

At the end of the day I feel blessed with so much riches of the soul.

Before retiring to bed I write down at least 5 blessings of the day.

Like thank you God for the gift of my family.

Thank you for giving me joy by helping an elderly woman.

Thank you for the beautiful sunset.

It soothed my heart.

I thank you for being aware to appreciate two people who felt special.

I heard beautiful chirping of the birds.

It was uplifting to my spirit.

And then I read a passage from any book that is pleasant.

Finally I listen to my loved one say good night and go to sleep soundly having placed my family, loved ones and the whole world in the hands of God the protector.

This daily gratitude ritual though simple gives me inner power and keeps me focused on my originality to serve others through the service of education.

Sun Set

You brought joy after the cloudy day.

You brought cheer on the faces of many.

How life giving your sunshine was!

Wonderful was your silver lining and colorful rainbows.

It brought joy to my gloomy day.

The sky looked so beautiful with your bright eyes.

What a sunshine it was!

The birds on the trees were chirping happily.

The butterflies were moving from one flower to the other.

What an excitement in their midst under the sunshine!

The rain

The rain is falling on the trees and the flowers.

Each drop looks like pearls on the leaves.

The birds on the trees are singing with joy.

The children under the trees are having fun.

What a cool rain!

The ants are running for their shelter.

The mother ants are leading the smaller ants.

The animals are heading towards home jumping and hoping with the melody of the rain.

What a beautiful rain!

The couples are sharing intimacy.

It's the time to share and care.

The elderly couples and children are walking on the ground enjoying to their hearts content.

What a graceful rain!

Evening walk

As I step out I feel the warmth of the setting sun with the silver lining.

I see people walking around with their loved ones enjoying each other's company.

The birds in the sky are flying in V formation heading towards their homes.

The people in the holy places are sitting and praying uniting their soul with the divine.

The sellers are calling out for ice-cream.

The children are worrying their parents to buy.

The boy in the street with the balloons is blowing high the bundle of it.

The tiny birds are fascinated as the balloon goes high.

They are lost in themselves in the mood of play.

The dog is barking and wagging his tail for his master who is busy chatting on the phone.

The lovers in the corner bench sharing intimacy.

The wind is blowing and touching them gently.

They are lost in their world of dreams.

The people passing by are a bit shy.

But they are blessing them in silence for their happy future.

The bagger woman is sitting with a bowl.

A girl passing by puts some money.

She smiles with joy like a sunflower with the tinkling sound of the coin.

The girl walks away home pleased to have made a day for someone.

The woman thanks God loudly for the kindness of the girl.

Truly they made a day for each other.

Still Night

How awesome is the still night with the millions of twinkling stars.

Nothing can be heard but one sound –

My own heart beat.

I hear it as I breathe in and breathe out.

What a miracle to be alive.

When thousands of people who have no chance to see another day.

Thanks do I give to the God of protector for surrounding me and you with his tender love in the still dark night.

Prayer of gratitude

When I wake up in the morning may I praise you for the gift of my life.

May I begin my day with your blessing.

With my eyesight may I see goodness in others and in all your created things.

With my nose may I breathe in love and breathe out peace.

My tongue may speak words of encouragement and appreciation.

Let my thought be positive and life giving to myself and to others.

When negative thoughts come may I change into positive thoughts.

May I hear your whispering sound in the blowing of the gentle breeze.

Let my ear hear your words of love being sung melodiously through the birds of the air and roaring of the waves.

When I hear painful stories of others may I listen attentively so that they may feel understood.

When I hear the unjust news may I be able to stand against it and take an action if possible.

When out in the garden may I feel your soothing touch through the green grass under my feet.

As I touch leaves on the trees and plants may I feel your cool healing hand.

When I carry a tiny baby in my arms let her feel the warmth of your love flowing through me.

Let an elderly person feel being led by you as I hold his hand to support.

Let my heart feel sympathy for the poor and the needy.

May I be a channel of your consolation to those sad and weary.

Let my heart spread your gentle love to everyone that I meet today.

Where there is hatred and misunderstanding let my heart be your bridge

May I surrender my family, loved ones, entire world and every activity that I do today into your loving care.

Moon light

What a charming beauty with the sliver spray around you.

You soothe the human hearts with your sparkling spray of light.

How awesome is the beauty of you.

The lovers are happy and enjoying deep moments.

For you are shading warm light upon them.

How lucky are the lovers under the shadow of your dim moon light.

Still I thank Thee

I give thanks to thee for the gift of my precious life.

Life though filled with the unexpected death of my dear father.

I discovered in the pain of loss the hidden quality of poetry unfolding more and more.

Penning down the emotions of grieve and hurt which can't be expressed to the human beings alone.

In the days of turmoil and confusion you held my hand and led me to the soothing green grass near the tiny stream.

Lost was I for the moment in your supernatural kingdom of peace.

Overwhelmed was I as pearls of tears ran down from my cheeks.

Counting the stars in the clear sky was a moment of deep consolation.

In it I felt the presence of mom and dad just like a child.

Relationship of new I built in prayer with them.

Felt affirmed of their constant and everlasting presence.

I believe in faith this existence of theirs in the twinkling bright stars for the moment.

I was held in your loving arms like a tiny babe in the moments of deep sorrow and anxiety.

Secure did I feel in your loving arms surrounded by your heavenly angles in the forms of humans.

Ever will I remember your blessings in the midst of pain.

You healed me from sickness through the caring touch of doctors.

Understood my situation of poverty and allowed me to have medicine without money.

How will I thank you God for your unfailing love for me?

Your face do I see and experience in my agents helping hand.

Your caring hand through human beings on my way of journey is unforgettable.

Fill me ever anew with your everlasting love.

May the New Year heal me completely from pain and sorrows.

May it unfold me your hidden surprises each new day.

May it be a significant and a memorable year for me and for my dear ones whom I hold close to my heart.

Out with the animals

Every afternoon I take our animals to the stream side to graze.

One is balcky and the other is browny.

Blacky is fat, strong and handsome.

He is brave and ready to attack the enemies.

He is the stronghold of the family to plough the field along with browny when the tractor is not available.

Bowny on the other hand is thinner than balcky but is same in height.

He is kind, courageous and strong.

When faced with danger he is ready to fight back other animals.

Both of them care for each other by licking and loving each other.

He is hard working along with blacky.

Both blacky and browny are bought from the market by my father as young calves.

Mother and father looked after them well.

Now they are in their prime youth.

Both of them are well trained by my father to work and to graze.

While grazing they don't harm others crops but graze on the field graciously.

While they graze I sit on the bank of the stream and listen to the gentle flow of water.

I touch it and put on my legs and hands.

I feel the coolness of it.

On the green grass I walk and feel it's softness.

Singing of the birds on the trees is simply delightful.

It is as though an orchestra is being played by the well known musician.

On the field I see the lush blooming flowers with colorful butterfly on it.

I think of the maker of all this and thank him for making it available to me freely and generously.

It reminds me of the hundred fold blessings of the creator.

His nature is to give and give abundantly.

I introspect my nature.

Deep inside I find riches stored in the forms of my strengths, abilities and talents.

I become aware of it and use it for the greater welfare of my family and the society at large as backy and browny with their physical strength.

Pre-lockdown

I went to three schools in search of job.

I had an interview in each of the school.

I was selected in Katherine Academy.

I was told by the Principal of the school to join on 30th of March 2020 followed by two days of seminar for the teachers.

I conveyed my good news at home and to my friend who congratulated me.

Dad was filled with joy and said to me let's rejoice your success.

To my bad luck after two days I received a call.

It was to say that the school is going to be closed due to Covid-19 hence lockdown for some time.

I started praying that the lockdown gets over soon but each time it increased.

I had no job of anytype.

I stayed at home and did the field work such as sowing, cutting of paddy, threshing and drying etc. along with my family.

In between I began taking tuition of some students for rupees hundred for a month.

But I was not paid well except for one or two months.

I started writing poems and posted to different websites in hope to win and get some cash.

But I didn't.

I was able to reach to the stage of semifinal only.

I didn't give up my hope.

I was happy that I was able to reach to the semifinal.

It gave me confidence and got encouragement for my writing skill.

In between I went to graze the animals to the stream side.

I sat and listened to the sound of the flowing water and gentle blowing of the breeze.

It soothed and consoled my lonely and jobless self.

I longed to get work but due to lock down I couldn't.

I thought of the possibilities to earn money but in the interior village it was impossible due to lack of job opportunities.

25th of July 2020 is never to be forgotten.

On this day my dad passed away.

It was a day filled with deep sorrow and pain.

My heart was broken and still is as I continue to miss his presence.

Dad was a supporter in every way may it be financially or seeing to the basic needs.

In his presence there was no fear of any kind.

He was like an evergreen tree giving fruit always.

I hope by next month school will reopen.

I look forward to be in the school and begin teaching with new zest.

May I be renewed in mind and heart in order to impart knowledge and value to the students.

Let my years in the school be a happy and fulfilling one.

Though I struggle with life I still give thanks to the God of all time who knows what is best for me.

Side of the road

I was laid in the dustbin beside the road.

The one who picked me up was a barren woman.

She rang her door bell.

At the sound of it I gave a loud cry with fear.

Her husband opened the gate gently and was surprised to see his wife having a baby girl in her arms.

For a moment he was speechless.

His wife narrated the story of how and where she found me.

Her husband patted me on my delicate cheek and took me in his arms happily.

He thanked God looking up above.

Late in the evening they went to the police station to report about me but no one claimed me even after a year.

They decided to have me as their first born baby given from the universe.

And they named me which means joy.

I was weak and looked frail.

Since they claimed me officially as their daughter they began treating me as their own baby.

They brought all the necessary things and clothing for me.

There was nothing less to cry about.

I grew up to three years old baby from a month old when I was found.

They decided to put me in the play school.

One fine day our young enthusiastic teacher gave us drawing papers and the crayons.

To my teachers amazement I drew myself, my present parents and the image of the one who laid me in the dustbin.

Her image resembled my pretty face but her eyes were filled with fear.

I colored her with the black crayons all over the body.

I was exhausted at the end of it.

My teacher observed me and let me color it until I was tired and satisfied.

Gradually my eyes were filled with tears.

She came close to me and hugged me tightly.

I sobbed and sobbed with the bitter feelings of being abandoned by my own mother.

Later I colored my present parents with bright color.

They looked happy and cheerful.

I went home and presented my painting to them.

While I tore and threw the one I colored in black.

What a joy to receive my painting.

My dad went and did the lamination of it and put it on the wall of our bedroom.

Mean while my mother hugged me in appreciation for it.

Eventually I began liking drawing and painting.

As years passed by lot of my emotional pain got healed through painting.

I enjoyed drawing and painting which was appreciated and encouraged by my parents.

My teachers too encouraged me always.

My original craft was revealed to me through the painful process.

Had I neglected I would have lost my true originality of to be a painter.

Beauty of creation

On the earth everything is perfect.

The ants are moving around freely.

The tiny birds singing away to their hearts content on the trees.

Some are swinging in their nests.

While others swimming in the stream on the piece of log.

How lovely is the creation of the creator!

The boys are grazing the animals in the green valley.

Their faces are lit up as though it is their dream job.

Sometimes they are calling out the animals by their names.

They are so happy to hear it as they look up to their masters with familiarity.

How beautiful is the instinct of understanding each other!

The sound of the music is clear and audible in the crowded street nearby.

The victory girls are dancing away with joy, creative steps and movements.

The bystanders are watching them with pride and awe as they clap their hands in rhythm to appreciate their success.

How good it is to celebrate their success!

Hero within

Peep inside.

Awaken the hero within.

Encourage him to become the master of his craft.

Let him bloom to his full capacity.

Fear not.

Walk alone.

You have a potential.

Live up to it.

Make a difference.

There is no other you in the world.

Life gets shorter with each passing day.

It's so true.

There was a lovely sunrise today.

So does a wonderful sunset with a silver lining above.

Darkness spread and soon the king of the day blew away.

With awareness live each day as though it is a last day.

For we do not know when the God of death will come knocking on our door.

Let the hero within live up to his potential.

And leave behind a legacy of his craft.

Gulmohar Tree

You remain nude for many months and look lifeless without leaves.

However you keep your hope alive.

You wait and wait in silence for the right time.

Gulmohar tree your spirit of endurance is inspiring.

You eventually sense some energy flowing in you.

The new shoots pop up.

You look tender and smooth at this stage of your life.

One wonders where you get the life from.

It's your deep rootedness to the earth I am sure.

You suddenly come of age.

You begin to dress up like an adult woman.

You then look elegant and gracious in your royal green and red attire of blooming flowers.

Like everyone you think of serving others.

You quench the thirsty birds with your sweet nectar.

You house many homeless creatures in your loving branches.

You soothe human hearts with your charming beauty.

Though you are a tree you serve others directly or indirectly.

Gulmohar tree your nature of giving freely is admirable.

Visiting aunt

My younger sister, nephew and myself set off to meet my unwell aunt.

On the way we talked about the memories of their childhood told by my dad.

By nature my aunt is hardworking and caring from the beginning.

She is the second one among the four siblings.

When we reached there she was overwhelmed to see us and her tears rolled down.

My younger sister and I held her.

All of us were in silence for sometime.

But we felt the energy of love and care passing through.

The heavy atmosphere became light.

To her bad luck her son and daughter in-law passed away some years back accidently.

She has a son who is into deep depression.

Her husband on the other hand is physically unstable due to fall.

The nephew is of eighteen years old tries to be of help to them.

In the midst of all the difficulties she keeps her spirit positive.

We washed her clothes and cleaned the house.

She felt fresh and clean.

By evening she told our nephew to make tea for us while we were still cleaning.

We sat together and had tea with sweet bread.

She looked peaceful and happy with our presence.

We promised her that she would be taken to the hospital tomorrow morning.

We wished them good bye and left for our homes leaving her in the care of nephew till the next morning.

I pray to God of health to restore good health to my aging aunt.

God of mercy have mercy upon the entire family.

May cousin brother find inner peace and be hopeful towards life.

Let uncle who is physically unstable due to fall become stronger.

God of Lenten season give them the grace to carry their cross as you carried.

Mother hen

Our mother hen named perseverance gave birth to 13 chicks on 13th of January in cold weather.

She was healthy but after hatching eggs her legs got paralyzed.

What's the reason we do not know.

She moves with the help of her upper legs now.

Sad I feel to see her struggling to balance her body.

When she was in good health she flew up to sit on our guava tree.

Along with her she accompanied our neighbouring hens too.

She was very influential then with her leadership quality.

My nephew is their care taker guided by my brothers.

Mother hen is gently lifted up and brought out in the sunlight by him.

The little ones come running after him.

He feeds them with ragi and water.

It is a beautiful sight to see him enjoying with them.

Sometimes he feels lazy to take care of them.

He requests me then to attend to them.

They don't come running after me as they behind him.

They are fond of him from the time they were just out of the shell.

He made a pretty home for them out of the cartoon box.

He put them in it every night to protect them from cold.

He demonstrated to me how he opens a tiny gate intelligently.

I appreciated his creativity and caring hand.

He felt great and proud and on the other hand I felt inner joy in appreciating him.

Other kids of his age too come and help him.

They love to be around the lovely little chicks.

Of course all feel sorry for the mother hen.

I notice that it is the chicks who are giving her life.

Though she struggles she keeps her hope alive.

Sometimes they sit on her back and other time rests under her wings.

So deep is her affection for them in-spite of ill health she lives up to her name.

Blue color

Blue is the color that I like most.

It's my favourite.

In it I look gorgeous and beautiful.

When I look up the sky I see the shades of blue combined with white.

Oh, it simply delights my heart and mind when it is combined with white and blue.

Blue is the color speaks of loyalty.

It's deep in color and beauty.

It's cool when out in the sun.

It's cooling to the eyes that see.

Though color it shapes my relationships with my loved ones.

It enables me to be loyal and true.

Blue is the color which symbolizes leadership quality.

It helps me to encourage, appreciate, listen and be a team builder wherever I am planted.

It enables me to rise up in the morning, do yoga, pray and begin my day with a grateful heart.

Blue is the color teaches me to lead my life.

Blue is the color that is serene and calm.

It enables me to be calm in moments of hardships.

It helps me to live a life that is serene and loving.

It's my constant companion as it soothes my heart with deep blue color.

Blue, oh, deep blue.

My desiring and most loved color with the combination of white.

An Engineer

His name means victory.

He is an independent oil engineer.

By nature he is optimistic, intelligent, hardworking, loving and loyal.

When he was in America he took a project for eighteen months in an Asian country.

He reached there and was warmly welcomed by his agent.

He began his project with enthusiasm and did his best before the company could come to inspect it.

To his bad luck the chemical that was supplied to him was not of standard.

His huge amount of money got drained in vain.

The situation was very pathetic.

He communicated the problem with the chemical suppliers but they did not do anything as it was supplied to him six months earlier.

He was tensed but looked for all the possibilities to solve the problem with a calm mind.

He didn't want to go back without completing the project on which he invested so much money.

He managed to get the other chemical with an agreement.

His agent was like a God sent angel to him.

He stood by him and looked for the ways to help him out.

He began working on his project along with his workers with a positive attitude.

He could not manage to have them longer due to shortage of money.

He started working day and night as he was working alone.

His life was very hard but he thought of his family who gave him inner strength to live.

In the course of time he did not have enough money to pay to the restaurant manager for his food.

He spoke to him and kindly agreed to give him food on credit.

In between he managed to pay him some amount for which the manager was happy.

Days arrived when he afforded to have only one meal a day.

His loved one was pained to know this but she could do nothing with the zero balance.

As days passed he began feeling weak as he was working hard with single meal a day.

After some months he got ill and was hospitalized.

He communicated this to his beloved who was far away.

She was stressed, sad and in pain.

She began praying for his good health day and night.

By God's grace he restored back his health.

He continues to work day and night with dedication and determination.

He hopes that his hard work will be blessed when the company will come to inspect it next.

He wants to make them feel proud of himself and his work when they come for the inspection.

In between he questions God for the hardships in his life.

However he takes this as a challenge and a trial time.

He constantly draws inner strength from the well spring of his heart which keeps him a tuned with the life of God.

His attitude of grateful heart for his ongoing project is admirable.

As per the meaning of his name he strongly believes to achieve victory over his hardship at the completion of his project.

So be it.

Stillness

In the moment of stillness I praise thee for obtaining me good health, peace of mind and hope.

Moment like this reminds me of God's goodness and caring hand.

I look within in stillness and find the authentic self hidden.

There is power within to change and recreate my better self.

There's clarity and possibility like never before in stillness.

I read books of inspiration and draw strength to live in the midst of turmoil and uncertainty.

Say good bye to negative thoughts and draw strength from positive words and phrases hidden in it.

It opens my heart and mind to the new possibilities of life.

Many have gone before like Mahatma Gandhi and Mother Theresa who acquired few possession of the world and looked vision filled with possibility to serve the world.

I draw strength from them to be of service to the world with my God given talent.

May I pen down words of power, strength and inspiration with each poem that I write and change the hearts of many.

Strength in prayer

Many sages, religious leaders and our great men woke up early morning everyday.

They spent time in solitude meditating and praying.

Some of the sages read the passage from Bhagwatgita and meditated on it.

They drew strength and power to reach the final goal of union with God through it.

While different religious leaders contemplated on the passage of their holy books.

They remained in silence and meditated on the words or phrase that touched their hearts.

They drew strength from it to live for the day and for their mission.

Political leaders of the past like Mahatma Gandhi, Abdul Kalam and Nelson Mandela have done the same.

They woke up at dawn and were in union with their God.

This sacred time of union with God strengthened them to carry out their big mission as leaders of their countries.

My own mother though ordinary woke up early.

She spent time in solitude praying for half an hour daily.

She had hardships in life but her prayer life strengthened her to take responsibility of the family courageously along with my father.

I had noticed her calmness in trouble.

It was the power of her daily union with God I suppose.

Would you like to wake up early and pray?

It's the sacred hour to reflect on life.

I am not lying you but only sharing the power experienced by our great leaders, sages and perhaps our own ordinary parents.

Let's make a first priority to begin our day in union with God for 5 minutes to begin with.

I bet you it is really strengthening.

It enables to get in touch with our true originality as to who we are and what is our purpose in life as pilgrims of the earth.

And of course give us strength to live for the day without any doubt.

Give a try.

Accident

I had a sugar from the time I was in my mother's womb.

Both my parents were teachers.

I was taken care of by both of them and in particular by my father.

I was a dotted daughter of his.

He cared and loved me more than my brother.

While coming to the school he would drop me in the car and go ahead to his school.

He would come at lunch break to make sure that I had taken an injection.

I was trained to do so from the time I was little.

My class teacher miss Anita accompanied me to the room near the staff room where I took injection regularly.

She would make sure I was safe.

I was an active student in the class.

I am friendly by nature and was close to my class teacher.

I loved to participate in all the class activities except sport due to my ill health.

Whenever we had class wise competition I would be the first one to take the responsibility and be of help to my class teacher.

Our school conducted many activities and competition for us on different occasions.

26th of January was approaching.

We were given class wise competition for the patriotic song.

As usual our class teacher prepared us well.

She told us to look for the T-shirts of flag color at home.

I looked for it but didn't find.

I took my father to the close by town to buy T-shirt for me.

We bought and were returning.

To our bad luck we met with an accident.

My father made sure I was safe.

I was unconscious while my father breathed his last.

Such great was his love for me.

I was brought home and my father was rushed to the near by hospital by the police.

But sadly he was already dead.

Everything was unbelievable.

I didn't know what was happening.

My school staff visited me along with the Principal.

It was consoling to my lonely heart.

My class teacher would ring me up and console me from time to time.

After a month I came to the school.

In the class my class mates and the class teacher was very sensitive.

In between she would give me time to share my pain.

I felt empty of not having him around anymore because I was close to him.

But with the passing of time I accepted his death.

37

I became independent and fearless.

I took responsibility to come to the school in the school bus.

Though painful I still thank God for everything.

He lived for a short time but poured his love on me like a due fall.

I shall ever cherish his love on my way of journey.

Prejudice

The year of golden jubilee was approaching in the school.

The big meeting was held in the staffroom in preparation for it.

Many ideas and thoughts were shared by different individuals as to how to celebrate this memorable event.

The programe was finalized by the Principal of the school.

The state wise cultural dance to be put up was approved along with other activities.

The lists of items were put up on the notice board attractively.

Each teacher had to choose the kind of dance she liked to teach her whole class and put a tick mark against it.

All the senior teachers went near the notice board and chose their favourite dances.

The junior teachers too chose and put a tick mark against it.

There was one dance left unnoticed by both the groups.

It was a tribal dance.

I stood silently near the notice board and put a tick mark against it.

While putting a tick mark I heard some ones voice.

I looked behind it was one of the senior teacher of the school.

Is there anything left for you she said.

I replied her saying yes and put a tick mark against it.

All the teachers went to their respective classes.

They told the students the name of the dance.

My students of grade sixth too were waiting eagerly.

I reached and entered the class.

In unison they asked me the name of the dance.

I told them the name of the dance which was a tribal dance.

On hearing this they said unhappily in one voice.

No we don't want to dance a tribal dance.

I asked them calmly to close their eyes and told them to get in touch with the reason for not wanting to dance a tribal dance.

After some time I told them to open their eyes.

I asked them to tell me honestly the reason for not liking a tribal dance.

Some of them said that the tribal people live in the jungle naked, they don't bathe and brush, they don't comb their hair and don't go to school.

While others said they are low and backward people.

I listened to each one of them attentively.

I thanked and appreciated their honest answer.

They felt pleased.

They agreed and nodded their heads while some said yes.

I told them the meaning of the tribal dance and the people in a gist.

Lastly I told them that your class teacher who you love and fond of is a tribal too.

Hearing this they felt very bad for their behavior.

And they said teacher you are not.

You don't look like a tribal.

But I am a tribal I said.

They asked forgiveness for not liking tribal people and for not wanting to dance.

They said to me from today we will love tribal people and our dance is going to be the best on the day of the golden jubilee of the school.

Being true to their word they practiced and it was one of the best dance performed by them with full gusto.

This group of students finished tenth grade but still keep in touch with me.

They are indeed special and transformed students whose mind is free from prejudice of tribal people.

I thank God for their honesty and freedom of expression.

It brought change in their way of looking at or perceiving tribal dance and the people.

Dream for the future

My nephew is eleven years old.

He is in standard six in St. Mary's English medium school Kuda.

He grew up in our home.

He is very fond of my mother and father who cared for him as a little boy.

He lives with his parents now.

But in holidays his home is our home.

When he was in U.K.G. he saw my uncle in his military uniform.

He looked at him standing like a mountain for his age.

He said to him grandpa when I grow up I will become like you.

The seed of his dream to become an army in future is growing day by day.

Now that he knows to surface internet he searches for the qualities and the education required for it.

He wrote down the list of it and showed me.

I wished him good luck and told him to work hard to reach his goal.

In the class he is the vice prefect.

He tries to take his responsibility well as narrated by his teachers.

On 26th of January and 15th of August he holds the flag of the country with pride and leads his class.

He is social, honest, brave and studious boy.

Though English is his second language he tries to pay attention in the class guided by his mother.

He knows and is aware of the financial problems of his parents.

Keeping this in mind he keeps his aim high.

This is the season of tamarind in the village.

On windy days he collects tamarind which is fallen from the tree.

He cleans it and goes to sell by himself to the village market.

It was so striking to see him buying a wrist watch for himself from the money that he sold.

Few days back he was asked by an uneducated parents to help their children to understand the question paper that was sent by the school.

He helped them willingly to understand the question paper as it is their second language.

Their mothers were so happy and told him that they will pay him Rs. 50 each.

He said to me with joy aunt, I will earn one hundred and fifty rupees for helping them.

I shall buy a torch for my parents with it.

When the electricity goes off they can use it.

What a thoughtful gesture at his young age.

He has a good circle of friends.

He is the leader in the group in the sense to take any responsibility for their picnic on 1st of January.

Though young he enjoys helping those in need.

He loves stories, playing football, cricket, swimming and watching patriotic movies.

I pray his original dream to become an army for the country may come true.

Father of the nation

The father of the nation we salute you.

We admire your inner power of calmness in the midst of big turmoil.

Great was your weapon of non violence with which you fought for freedom.

You were laden with the responsibility as a father and husband of your family.

Yet you found endless time for doing the service for the country as the leader.

Balanced was your mind and heart to give time generously for your family as well as for the country.

Rich were you in spirit of service and humility which became your sword to win the English with your peaceful mind.

Poverty was your dear and loveable friend after Kasturba your gentle wife who supported you silently.

Khadi was another weapon to drive away the invaders who ruled selfishly.

You understood the power of love through which you constantly drew strength from the well spring of your soul.

Deep was your life of contemplative prayer as you sat in stillness with closed eyes.

Married at the tender age with your wife yet you understood the responsibility of a family man.

Life wasn't easy for sure in fulfilling the family duties but heard and responded to a deeper call to be a leader of the country.

Tiny was your act of leaving another sandal when one was lost but profound was your thought behind it.

None can overpower your great humility, simplicity, depth and wisdom filled intelligence.

Leader of God sealed you with the natural leadership quality to be used for the nation which was under the British for two hundred years.

You lived your originality of to be a leader by becoming humble in great way.

There is no Mahatma like you in the whole of the universe.

You left behind a legacy of humble leadership to the nation.

Long live your soul in our country that was great then and always will be.

My mother

You woke up at the first cry of a cock.

You prayed quietly for some time.

You then started doing your house hold chores enthusiastically.

All the work was done by the time we woke up.

Mother how hardworking and devoted you were!

You went to the field to work untiringly.

You bent and took out weeds.

Your hands pained but didn't give up.

You cared for the plants as you cared for us until they were ready.

Some of your workers never felt tired of working with you.

They appreciated your kindness and love for they knew you treated them with dignity.

Mother how kind and respectful you were!

You cared for each of us.

You gave me bath cleanly.

You combed my hair and tied it up neatly.

You washed our clothes, dried and put them separately in our boxes.

You gave us food and fed us well.

You made sure that all of us were your healthy children.

Mother hats off to you for looking after five of us.

Mother how caring and loving you were!

Your expression of love to dad was searching and cooking the vegetables that he liked most.

You bought him time to time the clothes that he needed.

You waited for him to eat meals together.

Both of you worked and went everywhere together.

You looked after him well till your death in 2014.

Sometime both of you had some misunderstanding but forgave.

Mother how loyal and forgiving your heart was!

You are gone eternally leaving behind your loving memory.

We your children ever remember and cherish your love for us.

People still remember your kindness to them.

Many say she was very kind and loved me most.

My heart is filled with joy and pride to know you loved kindly.

Mother your name means kind and you lived up to it.

Long live your legacy of kindness and love in our hearts and in the hearts of those you touched!

Love for mission

Your name means father of speech or eloquent.

You were born in a simple middle class family in Rameswaram.

You had a humble beginning.

You sold news paper to make money to meet the needs.

Many books you read as a young growing up boy.

You had an observant eyes which spotted the birds soaring high into the sky, from this dream life came forth to become a scientist.

You were a bright student curious to know many things.

Your teachers instilled in you the value of desire and will which later helped you to fulfill your mission.

You woke up early and drew strength from the divine power for the day.

You had a great respect for self and others.

Your caring and social nature kept you bonded with your siblings.

You had a focused mind to contribute knowledge of science to the country and the world.

Your contribution in the area of science for the development of the country is incredible.

You were known then as a missile man and always will be.

Your contribution in the area of politics raised you to the ladder of committed President of India.

The people respected you and had a child like trust.

Though you were a bachelor you chose to live simply making science and politics as your mission.

In spite of being a great scientist and the president of the country you had few possessions.

This shows your victory over material things in the world of consumerism.

Few people understand the secret of being rich by having few possessions.

Mahatma Gandhi and Mother Theresa understood this secret.

They lived simply with high vision which raised them to the heights of sainthood.

You were a youth lover who saw in them boundless capabilities for the betterment of the country.

You visited the youth of the country and had a personal conversation with them.

Many were fond you including me.

You had an approachable personality due to which the youth came close to you.

You loved imparting knowledge of science to them untiringly.

You were called to the heavenly abode while lecturing to the youth in Shillong.

Sad we feel to say good bye to such a wonderful person like you.

At the same time we respect God's plan in your life.

He had a purpose of sending you to the world.

You lived up to your originality as a great scientist which was discovered by you at a young age.

You lived up to it hundred percent.

We salute you our admirable President and a missile man then and always will be.

Your love for mission in the area of science and politics will ever breathe life in the pages of history and in the hearts of human kind.

Sistine chapel

Michelangelo you were born with the exceptional gift of artistic mind and hand.

You finely painted each and every fresco on the ceiling.

You looked up untiringly with the paint and brush in your hand.

Some stuff and dust fell in your eyes but with a blink of a second you continued painting.

Though a sculpture you undertook the mission of mighty painting.

Each day was a new beginning.

You contemplated and imagined the image in your mind more than on the paper.

Each tiny part that you painted speaks of your whole attention.

One can never imagine as I can't even look up plainly for a minute.

The color of your choice speaks of your reflective soul.

Each fresco is painted deep, colorful and attractive.

The brush that you used was soft, hard and flexible.

The containers that you put in were adjustable.

The ladder on which you stood and sat was strong.

Every object that you used co-operated in unity with you.

Though back breaking you didn't give up in-stead painted for hours and hours.

While painting you entered the heart, mind and soul of the person.

This I know as I look up the ceiling with wonder and awe.

You painted for four years without a break.

How tiring to look and look every detail of it.

So much so that your eyesight got damaged.

Your dedication was outstanding.

Michealangelo blessed are you among all the other artists of your time and now.

Legacy you left behind of your craft of art.

Indeed you gave birth to a magnificent fresco of Sistine chapel.

Long live your name in the history of all ages.

Faith

Her parents were married for twenty years.

They had a dream of having a baby just like any other couples.

Months passed by but no sign.

Year after year they longed to have at least one baby.

But they could not.

God had his own plan.

Her father turned fifty five and her mother forty five.

One fine day they visited a shrine of Our Lady in Haregaon in Ahmednager district.

They prayed to Mother Mary with an unwavering faith to conceive a baby.

They burned a candle at her feet.

They returned home and after few days they were surprised to know that she was expecting a baby.

They were overwhelmed with the mercy of God and the grace of mother Mary.

They went back to the shrine to show gratitude to her by burning eleven candles at her feet.

Both of them were happy to have her at their lap which was empty for two decades after their wedding.

They named her which means prayer.

She is the apple of their eyes.

She loves Mother Mary as her own parents.

She is a gift of God through Mother Mary to her parents.

She says she shall ever love and serve God and Mother Mary through her act of service.

As I listened to her story of how she came to this world I was speechless.

I could only thank God and Mother Mary for the gift of her.

I rejoice with her parents for her existence in the world.

She through her moving story has a big mission to inspire others to grow in faith.

A faith which can't be seen or touched just like the wind but can be felt with the inner eye of the heart as experienced by her parents.

Passing away

Our mother hen was found dead this morning.

My nephew stood speechless in front of her who took care of her and the chicks always.

With a very sad voice he announced her death.

I heard and went near it and felt very sad thinking of the little chicks who are still tiny.

Both of us stood in silence for sometime as the atmosphere was gloomy.

He took out the little chicks hiding.

They didn't see her mother's dead body as it was quickly hidden from them.

We dug a hole in the back of our garden and buried her.

He and his friends too felt sorry and sympathized him.

I realized every passing away is painful no matter who it is.

During the entire day the little ones ran here and there not realizing their mother's death.

Late evening when the time came to be inside the house they missed her terribly.

They cried and cried looking for her.

Somehow we managed to put them in their house.

Till late night they were restless not wanting to sleep.

I went and peeped at them.

The slightly older chicks carried the younger ones on their back.

It was a beautiful insight of being responsible as an older sibling.

Gradually they fell asleep putting their heads on each other.

In the morning they were out in the sunlight.

They pitifully ran here and there in search of her but they never found.

She is no more.

But everyone remembers the mother hen for her leadership quality, persevering spirit and her caring nature.

Unique Taj

TajMahal you are one of the seven wonder of the world.

In it we find true love between Shah Jahan and Mumtajmahal.

Shah Jahan so deep was your love for her that you built a Tajmahal in her name.

Alive and strong it remains in the eyes of generation to generation.

Strong was your love for her that you spent time in planning and designing a resting place.

Incredible in the history of India and of the world is this place.

It is a symbol of your everlasting love for her.

One can imagine how lost and lonely you felt in losing her.

Day and night you spent in love and harmony.

There was no time lived without thinking of each other.

You loved her and she loved you.

Truly both of you were made for each other for life eternity.

Shah Jahan you made impossible possible.

Took long years of twenty two to complete but you didn't give up.

Precious and best of things and material you used.

It stands out in the whole of the universe as a unique Taj.

You called men from far and wide to design it.

Each person put in his best to complete the Tajmahal.

Workmen of many in numbers toiled day and night to make it outstanding.

You buried her remains in the garden close to Tajmahaal till you completed it.

So constant and strong was your love for her.

At the completion of it you took her remains to Tajmahal giving her a resting place for eternity in the hands of the Lord.

You are not here nor she today.

But her name and yours continue to breathe in the heart of Tajmahal.

Your intimate love for her is hidden in Taj is a legacy of your deep love for her.

Long live legacy of your unconditional love for your wife Mumtaz in Tajmahal.

You inspire me with your beauty, meaning and wonder when I see.

Let it be contagious to those visiting Tajmahal to love loyally to their life partners.

May unique Tajmahal continue to stand erect and strong to witness love to the next generation in the years to come.

Banker to teacher

Her name means unique.

She grew up in Mumbai in a wealthy family.

Her parents were both working.

They allowed her daughter to become what she wanted.

After finishing tenth standard with a very good percentage she went in to the stream of commerce.

In the college she was one of the bright one among the others.

She was elegant and had a soft corner for the poor students of her class.

During the lunch break she would look out for them and give them some money to eat in the canteen.

She had a good circle of friends matching her social nature.

When she finished collage she did banking and became a bank manager.

Since she was from well to do family she lacked nothing.

She started earning plenty of money but somehow she was unhappy.

Something was still missing in her life.

What was it?

One day she was conversing with her close friend.

She happened to narrate this to her.

She suggested her to spend some quiet evening alone at the beach.

Though reluctant and not very happy to be alone at the beach she decided to go.

She took with her a pad and a pen.

She observed everyone passing by.

She watched at the sea gulls enjoying in the water.

As she was looking at them a question came to her mind which would entirely change her profession later.

What makes the sea gulls so happy?

It's the water in the sea she says.

They are at the right place where they are suppose to be originally.

She took out her yellow cover pad and a blue pen.

She looked at the colorful setting sun which led her to still her mind and heart.

She wrote.

What makes me happy?

She recalled her childhood when she enjoyed teaching two poor kids who lived close to her apartment.

Again she wrote.

Teaching makes me happy.

She enjoyed teaching others as a kid and it was her original profession in fact which she had not paid attention to all this while.

The moment she realized this originality of herself she decided to resign as a bank manager and went to the stream of teaching.

She completed her B.ed and applied in the school.

She was appointed as a teacher and became a class teacher of seventh standard.

She loved students and the students were very fond of her.

In the staff she was social and a team builder.

In few months she became well known in the school for her social and enthusiastic nature to teach.

Since she was a responsible person the management found in her a trustworthy teacher.

After two years of teaching she was given the position of a vice principal by the management.

She is very happy in the teaching line like that of sea gulls when she had watched alone that evening.

Dream of that night

She sits still in the corner with her head bent low.

I go close and try to greet her.

She does not look up but says good morning in a faint voice.

I sit next to her and make a conversation.

In the course of it I come to know her mother's sudden death.

She was close to her mother than her father.

In her she found a friend to play with and to study.

Her world is broken ever since her mother passed away.

At times she visits the graveyard and spends five to ten minutes praying to her.

Solace she finds praying to her in agony.

She returns from the graveyard with a light heart.

She meets her father and tells him how happy she is after visiting her mother.

He feels emotional and tears of joy and pain flows from his cheeks.

He hugs her daughter and affirms her presence.

That evening both of them feel inner joy unlike other days.

Father cooks that night delicious food for her daughter.

They have early dinner and go to sleep peacefully.

Her daughter wakes up suddenly in the middle of the night.

She finds her mother in a dream.

Her mother is very much alive in her dream.

She sees her wearing a wedding gown which she wore for her wedding day some years back.

Her mother sits with her father and they chat endlessly.

They chat about the present, past and the future.

They are concerned about the future of their daughter.

While talking her mother suddenly disappears.

She could see her no more and feels sad but hopeful.

Her father consoles her and she sleeps soundly till the morning.

She feels as though she really met her mother in her dream that night.

Her mother lived as a loving mother and a faithful wife to her husband.

She is no more with them but still remember her love and faithfulness which is engraved in their hearts.

Lover of nature

You were born to your wealthy father and mother in Assisi.

Mother was tender and loving cared for you untiringly.

Father who had a possession looked forward to make you wealthy like him.

But someone had a desire to make you follow him in great poverty.

You grew up close to the hill surrounded by gorgeous nature.

You enjoyed horse riding along with your cousins and friends.

You had a heart for friendship with boys and girls especially with Clare whom you admired and adored as your girl friend.

You met her in the midst of blooming flowers in the specious field and spent moment of joy.

You heard a call to religious life in your prime youth.

You responded generously without a thought of turning back.

Though hard for sure to live a life of religious but bore everything for the love of the one who called you.

Founder were you of your congregation with courage, simplicity and dedication.

Poverty was your most dear and loveable friend.

You clothed yourself with the humble poverty of sack.

You gathered wealth of heaven while living on earth.

Your inner being was surrounded with positivity and energy.

Sent out that energy and positivity that was contagious and healthy.

Had a great mind filled with wisdom and intelligence.

You won the heart of Pope with your poverty and intelligence.

None had the spirit like yours which was crowned by your loveable companion poverty.

Melted his heart and gave you the permission to begin a new order of Franciscan.

You saw and experienced the presence of God in nature.

You called lovingly by name to the moon sister and to the sun a brother.

Birds of the air understood the language that you spoke to them.

They surrounded you with their cheerful presence.

When you slept on the hill facing the blue sky you felt grateful to the maker of nature.

The rustling of the leaves with the gentle breeze was soothing to your heart as you sat for meditation.

Many you inspired and touched to live a life of poverty including Clare.

Your humble service to the lepers was an act of deep humility and learning for others.

Rich were you in every way but your richness didn't affect your service to those dying lepers.

Human dignity you gave them which was like a healing balm.

Let your name St. Francis of Assisi be ever sung and adored by the birds of the air, flowers of the field and humans of the earth.

May you fire us with your zeal to take care of the nature as you did in the 13th century.

Lawyer to writer

You were born to a good and value based parents.

You were a bright student who possessed leadership quality than other students of your class.

You had a humble beginning who walked up the ladder of success as a young lawyer.

Indeed you were one of the best lawyer of the time.

You earned pots of money, had a beautiful house, lovely wife and the expensive red ferrari.

The time of enjoyment reached to the heights with your hard work.

Gradually you felt more and more drawn to your work forgetting the affection and the time that needed your family especially your wife and the kids.

The time came when your wife decided to stay separate and eventually got divorced.

You went through turmoil and deep depression.

It was a world of darkness altogether.

You had a good circle of friends but they too had no time for you.

You felt lonely and drunk day in and day out.

Gradually your health deteriorated.

A day came when you collapsed in the court while fighting a case.

It was the time of new beginning in your life.

You left the old and embraced a new.

You had no one to turn to by this time.

Your beloved wife was no more with you and your gem like kids.

It was the time of deep loneliness.

You had no meaning left in life.

At this time with the suggestion of one of your friend you attended the seminar.

You sensed back some meaning in life.

You resigned from a reputable lawyer and headed towards the East in search of new meaning in your life.

You met Sadhus who listened to your success and deep sorrow of your life.

They guided you to find true meaning in life.

You were at peace and content with yourself.

You promised them to share the knowledge received by them to the rest of the world.

You started sharing this precious knowledge through writing and conducting leadership seminars.

Today you enlighten the hearts and minds of many through your passion of writing and conducting leadership seminars worldwide.

You discovered your originality of to be a writer instead of lawyer.

You enjoy writing books after books for the people to be inspired by your thoughts and knowledge received.

Your name means fame or bright.

You live up to your name.

You are one of the best speaker and writer of the 21st century.

My father

You were born to your humble parents Joel K. and Monica.

Little were you when you lost your dear mother as you hold only a faint memory of her.

Sad you felt as you recalled her later in life.

You and your kid brother was looked after by your elder siblings who when you remembered tears of gratitude welled up in your eyes.

You had a simple beginning as your father was laden with the responsibilities as a young widower.

Sometimes you had very little food to eat with rice water but love was strengthening.

Days of school in St. Joseph Torpa was with one uniform.

Sandal was of leaves stitched by your own hands to protect yourself from heat.

No electricity so your study hour was on the way on foot six kilometers away from home.

Sacred you kept this hour of study obedient to your elders.

Though poor you were bright and responsible student trusted by your teachers.

A blessed day arrived which would improve your life of poverty.

It was the day when a team of military men came to the school to recruit boys to military.

The teacher gave first priority to the poor and the bright students of the class.

So you were one of them poor, smart, tall, well built and good at sport.

You were selected at the age of seventeen though under age.

You took life seriously to climb the ladder of success.

Though tough to undergo training encouraged and supported by your father you took an oath as C.R.P.F with honesty and dedication.

The value of truth and selflessness was at the center of your heart in your life of service.

Gifted with the good communication skill you had a desire to become a lawyer but poverty was so great to overcome.

However you put this into practice after retirement as a member of the village Panchayat Samiti.

Where you got ample of opportunities to guide and lead the village into right direction by solving problems that would arise from time to time.

A guide were you to the younger generation by sharing with them your wisdom and knowledge.

Loss do they feel and grieve for your absence in their midst.

You were close to my mother and worked hard together in the field yielding crops in abundance.

You shared with the less privileged from time to time who remember your generosity and kindness with a grateful heart.

Dad we remember and cherish your loving care, encouragement, appreciation, guidance and support.

I personally miss our time of sharing our dreams and analizing it.

Sitting beside you listening to your life experiences were moments to be remembered always.

I miss your gentle voice calling me out as Anita with tender love.

We pained you knowingly and unknowingly.

Forgive us dad our heart sobs in the still night for there is a big vacuum not having you.

My heart was filled with sorrow to see you suffering with an unbearable pain for one and a half day.

I begged mother Mary to heal you but in no way.

Dad you breathed last on 25th of July 2020 kissing the cross of your rosary peacefully.

You met God and our dear mother who is in heaven before you.

There is emptiness within and out as we are left two yet to be settled.

Though you are not around your gentle voice resound in my ears and deep in my lonely heart.

Dad you are gone but your legacy of selfless service and tender love continue to live in our hearts.

Simple woman

Mother Theresa you were born to a lovely devoted couple.

A mother who instilled in you the value of charity.

And father who died when you were a kid of eight gave you unwavering faith in God.

At young age of twelve you felt the call to religious life.

You went to Ireland to join the sisters of Lourato when you turned eighteen.

You made a commitment to God and served him through the service of education.

You felt call within a call while traveling to Himalaya in the train for retreat.

It was a tiny whispering of God to which when you responded grew like a mustard seed.

There and then you decided to leave the Lourato congregation and started a new order of missionary of Charity.

You felt drawn by the poor and the marginalized of Kolkata and settled there to serve them.

In them you saw none but Christ.

You were ready and willing to walk miles for the poor and the destitute.

So much so that you were spit on the palm of your hand while asking for money for your people.

Though you were insulted you never gave up instead gave another hand to beg.

This humble gesture of yours moved the man to become a new.

Your life of prayer and adoration gave you the strength to love those wounded and dying people.

You were a loving heart to all who never felt anyones love except rejection.

How happy they were to receive your affection which was like a healing balm.

You dressed simply with a plain white blouse and blue boarder sari.

It was so simple in appearance but it looked rich in your glowing face.

Your humble service reflected your inner beauty in your whole being.

Your wealth was love free for all human kind.

There were moments of darkness in your life where you never felt the presence of God.

It was a time of long duration filled with the experience of desolation but you never gave up your hope and trust in God.

You received noble peace prize for your dedicated work on earth and in heaven a crown of sainthood.

You were great in every way.

You were great to serve the poor, wounded and the dying.

Initially I could not even manage to see the deep wounds of those dying people as a B.ed student for our outreach programme .

Hats off to you saint Mother Theresa for giving yourself whole heartedly in the service to the least of the society.

Gratitude do I render to God for being an example and for your dedicated work.

Legacy you left behind of your humble service to the world which will reign forever.

Living funeral

I feel unwell a bit for the past few days.

So I decide to have a living funeral of mine in my home.

I invite all my near and dear ones.

I don't tell them the secret of get together until they come home.

I keep a surprise of our get together.

They arrive one by one.

All of them are curious to know about the purpose of get together.

There is joy and laughter as they wish each other including me.

They ask about the purpose of our get together.

Living funeral of mine I say politely.

All get shock of their lives hearing this.

I explain to them about the purpose of my living funeral.

I tell them when I die I won't hear all the good things that you will say about me.

So I would like to hear it now while I am alive and tell you as well.

I had not been feeling well these days.

I don't know how long I will live.

That's the reason I called for the get together.

That's a very good idea and wise one.

We are glad.

Let me tell you how much you mean to us.

Personally I would like to thank you for your love, care and support that I have experienced.

You are gentle, loving and a loveable person.

I remember always your loving concern that you showed me after my father death.

Thank you so much.

What I want to tell you is you are blessed with the gift of mind and heart.

You are approachable and have a deep listening heart.

When I was going through hard time you listened to me attentively.

I felt understood and cared for.

Thank you for that I will never forget.

For me you are a guide and a friend.

You taught me to speak in English.

I am not afraid or shy to communicate with others in English.

You also gave me your precious time when I was going through emotional pain.

I felt light and peaceful after sharing with you.

Thank you so much from the depth of my heart.

What I want to tell you is you are a brave woman who is not afraid of death but is preparing her good bye.

It shows your bravery and preparedness for death.

Honestly you are poetic, reflective, artistic, kind, helpful, intelligent, beautiful, hardworking and able to sing and dance.

You appreciate others by writing poems on their birthday is a beautiful gesture.

Keep it up!

We don't want you to die now.

For me you are a family holder.

Your attitude towards life is positive even though you tend to become negative sometimes.

You are able to shift your mind from negative thoughts to positive.

Your forgiving heart is inspiring and contagious to those living around.

Your love for teaching, nature and time of solitude is incredible.

Thank you for being an inspiration for me.

All of us would one by one continue telling you how much you mean to us.

But due to time limit since it is getting late night we can't proceed.

However each of us wants to affirm all the good qualities mentioned by others.

Our heart is heavy and is in deep pain to say good bye to you.

We love you and want you to live many more years.

Get well soon!

After hearing all of you I have no words to say.

I am really speechless.

I feel overwhelmed, loved and special.

I feel valued and my life meaningful.

Before we depart I want to say a big thank you to each of you for your appreciation, affirmation and for being there as part of my life.

May we praise, appreciate and encourage one another while we live and not wait for the funeral day only.

Truly it is uplifting and healing as I have experienced with the depth of my heart today.

At every funeral one question always strikes me.

That is.

What do I want people to remember me for when I die?

Final destiny

As I reflect on my existence in the world I become aware of the reality of death as well.

Every funeral reminds me that I have come to this world as a pilgrim for some years.

I become aware that I am made of dust and I shall return to the dust.

But the spirit within me will never die.

This truth gives me zest to live my life meaningfully and happily.

While I live on this earth I want to contribute to the world in some way as others have to make a better place.

Mahatma Gandhi made our county a better place by giving us freedom.

On the other hand Mother Theresa through her humble service to the least of the society.

Abdul Kalam made a better place through his contribution in the area of science and politics.

While Nelson Mandela by giving freedom to his people in-spite of being jailed for 27 years.

Though they are dead their contribution to the country and the world is always remembered.

They have left their legacy of untiring service to the country and the world at large.

What is my role?

All of us can't be great leaders or big persons to make a contribution to the world.

As for me I am an ordinary teacher by profession.

So I try to be the best teacher by preparing the students best citizens of the future of the country.

I try to be their guide and a friend by giving them academic knowledge as well as value based life.

I become aware of my big responsibility as a teacher to mould life or to destroy it.

So keeping this in mind I try to encourage and appreciate their good qualities.

It lifts them up and they feel special.

On their birthdays I write simple appreciative poems about them and give them as birthday gifts.

What a joy on their faces when they receive it!

You might wonder and say.

How will I make a contribution to the world with my small work?

Yes you can hundred percent.

Suppose you are a sweeper.

When you sweep the road and empty the dustbin you are making our surrounding clean.

You help to stop spreading many harmful diseases and protect the environment from pollution.

People feel fresh and clean to walk or to move around and do their work.

So remember through any profession you can make a contribution to the world.

Only you have to become aware of it by asking yourself two questions.

Who am I?

Why am I here for in the world?

When you introspect and reflect on these two questions it will enable you to get in touch with your originality of who you are and what you are meant to be.

Once you become aware of it, live your talent hundred percent for the betterment of your family and for the welfare of the society at large.

One day you and I will be called to enter our final destiny of death.

Remember though ordinary you are unique and special.

So live your original craft in such a way that your name will be written in the pages of history or in the hearts of humankind in a big or small way.

This will be a reward or an award for you from the universe for your good work on earth.

About the author

Anita Kongari was born and brought up in a lovely village called Urikel Barka Toli, situated in Jharkhand. It is positioned

at the foot of a hill surrounded by beautiful nature. The poet graduated from Primary and Secondary school in Jharkhand and Higher education in Mumbai. She has completed B.ed and M.A in History through Mumbai University. She is a teacher by profession. She loves to be in the midst of students. She likes to pen down simple poems that flows from her heart. She enjoys nature and a time of solitude. She likes reading a variety of books.

Summary of the book

This book contains poems on different themes. In some, the reader will learn to love and respect themselves and others. While in others, the reader will find joy in appreciating people. In some of the poems, the reader will discover inner power in stillness and solitude. It will also unfold to the reader - richness in the attitude of daily gratitude. Finally, it will enable them to live their original craft fully and leave their legacy as per God's given talents. Even if the reader may be gone one day, his name will live forever in the pages of history or in the hearts of humankind in a big or small way.

www.ingramcontent.com/pod-product-compliance
Ingram Content Group UK Ltd.
Pitfield, Milton Keynes, MK11 3LW, UK
UKHW040009200726
13854UKWH00001B/106

9 789354 724497